D0977027

A BOOK OF CUT FLOWERS

BY
SHEILA OKUN

ILLUSTRATIONS BY MARY CLOSE

William Morrow and Company, Inc.
New York
1983

A QUARTO BOOK

Library of Congress
Catalog Card Number: 82-62586

ISBN 0-688-01971-4

A Book of Cut Flowers
was produced and prepared by
Quarto Marketing Ltd.
212 Fifth Avenue, New York, N.Y. 10010

Editor
Bill Logan
Art Director/Designer
Richard Boddy

Typeset by BPE Graphics, Inc.
Color separations by
Hong Kong Graphic Arts Service Center.
Printed and bound in Hong Kong by
Leefung-Asco Printers Ltd.

Second Printing

CONTENTS

ACACIA
AGAPANTHUS
ALLIUM
ALSTROEMERIA
AMARYLLIS
ANEMONE
ANTHURIUM
ANTIRRHINUM
ASTER
ASTILBE
BELLS OF IRELAND
BIRD-OF-PARADISE
BOUVARDIA
BRODIAEA
CATTAILS
CELOSIA
CENTAUREA
CHRYSANTHEMUMS
    SPIDER
    FOOTBALL
    OTHERS
DAHLIAS
DAISY
DELPHINIUM
DIANTHUS
EREMURUS
EUPHORBIA
FREESIA
GERBERA
GLADIOLUS
GLADIOLUS, MINI
GLORIOSA ROTHSCHILD
GODETIA
GYPSOPHILA
HELICHRYSUM
HELICONIA

HYACINTHUS
IRIS
KNIPHOFIA
LIATRIS
LILAC
LILIUM
    CONNECTICUT KING
    & RED KNIGHT
    ENCHANTMENT
    RUBRUM
LIMONIUM
LUPINE
MARIGOLD
MONKSHOOD
NARCISSUS
NERINE
ORCHIDS
    ARACHNIS
    CYMBIDIUM
    OTHERS
ORNITHOGALUM
PEONY
PHLOX
PHYSALIS
PINCUSHION FLOWER
POPPY
PROTEA
ROSES
SOLIDAGO
STOCK
THISTLE
TUBEROSE
TULIP
YARROW
ZANTEDESCHIA
ZINNIAS

INTRODUCTION

When my partner and I were studying landscape design, we hardly expected we would become florists. In those days— less than a decade ago—the average flower shop was three-fifths ferns and baby's-breath, one-fifth daisies and mums, and another fifth assorted roses, gladiolus and corsage flowers. Only the rich could get bird-of-paradise and spray orchids, poppies and irises, Rubrum lilies and gloriosa rothschild. All that has changed. Better distribution—chiefly from the gigantic flower markets near Amsterdam in Holland—has more than doubled the number of beautiful species readily available. Our International Flower Market, and other shops like it, show this change to advantage, selling as wide a variety of species as possible at a reasonable price per stem. The flowers are set out in the store for anyone to touch and smell. We do weddings, funerals, and other occasions, but we specialize in flowers for everyday enjoyment. We like to let people choose their own combinations and imagine their own arrangements. I have written this book to show just how wide and lovely a selection there is, and to give you a few ideas of how to use it.

Flower arranging is not nearly so difficult an art as some imagine. Most people have enough native good taste and familiarity with their environment to make pleasing and appropriate arrangements. As with any art, there are basic techniques which you need to know in order to begin.

When you purchase flowers, be sure that the ones you buy are fresh. To determine how fresh a flower is, look over the leaves. If they are turning yellow or spotting, it is a sure sign of age. Shaking a flower *gently* will also help you judge its freshness, since petals will fall if the flower is old. Try to buy flowers as close to bud stage as possible, since they will last longer. Buds will open up within a day if placed in warm water after being recut.

Any number of old wives' tales tell how to keep flowers fresh: recommendations include adding a pinch of sugar, two aspirin or a penny to the water. None of these are effective. The best methods are to use floral preservative or a few drops of bleach or soda pop. Each acts as a bactericide. But perhaps the easiest way to keep flowers fresh is to start out with a clean container, change water daily and frequently recut the stems.

When you have chosen your flowers and are ready to arrange them, prepare both stems and water. Cut the bottom of the stems with a sharp knife, not a scissors, slicing on an angle to provide more surface for absorption of water. All foliage should be removed from the lower part of the stem as otherwise it will decay and create bacteria in the water, clogging the stems and inhibiting their ability to draw water. All flowers—with the exception of irises, which must always be put in cold water—do best when placed in lukewarm water.

Healthy flowers aside, the most important element in any flower arrangement is the device that holds it together. Probably the most common and versatile of support devices is the pin holder, or frog. It can be found in all sizes and shapes, but the most practical sizes are those between two and three inches (3–8 cm) across. Waterproof clay, which is reusable, should be used to affix the pin holder to the bottom of the container.

Probably the next most popular holding aid is Oasis, or floral foam. It is sold in bricks or blocks in flower markets. Soaked for even a few minutes in water, it will supply moisture to the flower stems for several days. But note that some flowers with soft stems, such as gerberas and anemones, don't do well in Oasis: the tips of the stems become clogged.

Whether you use a pin holder or foam, place the stems as close together as possible without crowding them. Try to cut stems to unequal lengths or add ones of the same length at different angles so they don't all appear to be the same height. Additional interest can be gained by using flowers at different stages of development, particularly buds, and by facing the flowers in different directions.

One can also keep flowers in place by using wire netting. Chicken wire works well in tall containers and will support heavy stems. Once the wire is wedged inside the container, it can be left in place and reused. The most beautiful means for holding stems, particularly in glass containers, are small river rocks or pebbles, which add color and texture to the inside of the container and can be used to hide a pin holder. Clear glass marbles or chips look well used in the same way in contemporary designs.

Even the most unconventional or ultramodern arrangement in some way organizes the material and employs simple elements of design. Color commands attention most forcefully, so care should be taken to select materials of compatible hue. Line and pattern must also be considered. Balance is an integral part of the arrangement; it is established by the placement of the main stem or vertical axis and the relationship or distribution of the other flowers around it. Larger or darker flowers tend to establish weight at the base, where it belongs, and smaller, light-colored flowers may be placed higher up in a design.

Proportion is another factor that greatly influences the success of the arrangement: the height and width of the flowers should be one-and-one-half to two times that of the container. Although there are exceptions to this rule—it can be altered, for example, by extending the arrangement down the sides of the container—it's a good rule of thumb to use when deciding what quantity of flowers to buy.

Mass arrangements are typically full and contain a fair

quantity of similar material. The flowers usually radiate from a central point, and the overall arrangement has a recognizable shape, such as round, triangular, or fan. The design evolves from the use of background materials, called "filler," chosen for their similarity, and striking flowers that are repeated to serve as focal points.

Modern art has a profound effect on flower arranging, and modern arrangements reflect this influence. Fewer flowers are used, and natural forms are altered by knotting, bending or clipping stems, foliage and branches. Exaggerated proportions and exotic materials surprise the eye, and the bold forms and sharp contrasts excite interest.

Ikebana, or Japanese floral art, has also influenced flower arranging, especially modern designs. Though the use of plant material may be sparing, a sense of harmony prevails. Balance is based upon the Oriental *yin-yang* approach to the phenomena of nature and is very orderly and controlled. There are numerous schools of *ikebana*, such as Nagiere, Rikka, Shoka and Moribana. The enthusiastic flower arranger can learn to experiment with classical *ikebana* or with one-, two- or three-flower designs.

For both Western and Eastern design, another important consideration is foliage. Leaves, bare branches and berry-covered branches are indispensable as filler to enhance your design. Consider lemon leaves, ti leaves, and the foliage of eucalyptus, pittosporum and ruscus, in addition to the more traditional Baker and asparagus ferns. Experiment with different materials, and don't hesitate to pick up an interesting branch and prune it to suit your needs. First and last, flower arranging should be an expression of your own sense of fun and artistry.

Sheila Okun
New York

ACACIA

WATTLE
MIMOSA
(A. decurrens dealbata, A. longifolia)
(Family: *Leguminosae*)

The flowers on a stalk of acacia resemble a large version of the blossoms of baby's-breath. The sunny, yellow, ball-shaped flowers are small and fluffy and have a dainty, aetherial quality. They look beautiful with white or other yellow flowers. Available only for a short time during the autumn, they are a good filler flower or can be used by themselves as a striking accent in a shiny black vase. Inexpensive and relatively long-lived, they are a delightful addition to any bouquet.

AGAPANTHUS

LILY OF THE NILE
(A. africans, A. umbellatus)
(Family: *Liliaceae*)

❧

The stark, dramatic appearance of the agapanthus
makes it an excellent choice for a contemporary
setting. The long stalk is topped by a cluster of about
100 flowers which bloom successively over three or
four days. This dynamic feature makes the
agapanthus long-lived, since the old blossoms can be
pinched off without adversely affecting the health or
appearance of the flower. Available in blue or white,
these flowers with their large round heads perched
on trim leafless stalks have a bold but airy quality
that lightens the air of a summer's day.

ALLIUM

ONION FLOWER
(A. albopilosum, A. christophii)
(Family: *Alliaceae*)

❦

When you need an outstanding flower for a summer
arrangement, the Giant allium is a dramatic choice.
Its dense, round head, up to ten inches (25 cm) in
diameter, is made up of myriad little, star-shaped
lavender flowers, all set upon a tall, leafless stem.
Eremurus, liatris and lilies make fitting partners for
the onion flower, though it also stands well on its
own. Try cutting the stems to different heights for a
balanced, but striking single variety design. If the
flowers you choose have small, flattened areas on
their heads, don't worry: The trick to fluffing them
up is to hold the sturdy stem upside down and roll it
quickly between your palms.

ALSTROEMERIA

PERUVIAN LILY
(A. pelegrina, A. aurantiaca)
(Family: *Liliaceae*)

~

Alstroemeria is hardly impressive in itself, but it is an exquisite and versatile flower for your arranging palette. Available in pink, apricot, salmon, red, lilac, yellow and cream—streaked or dappled with white, green or beige—its clustered flowers blend with virtually any partner. The unassertive, delicate trumpets set off more dramatic flowers like showy lilies, godetias, gerberas, or irises. Cheap, always available and quite long-lived, it is among the most popular flowers in any market.

AMARYLLIS

BELLADONNA LILY
(A. belladonna)
(Family: *Amaryllidaceae*)

~

The sturdy grace of Virgil's shepherdess, Amaryllis,
is reflected in the erect and recurved blossoms of the
flower that bears her name. Though others—notably
the grosser, more symmetrical hippeastrums—are
also called amaryllis, they cannot match the delicacy
of the belladonna lily. It shares the studied
nonchalance of the alstroemeria, with its six to
twelve flowers clustered irregularly at the head of the
stem, but the rose, pink or red of amaryllis cannot
be matched by the humbler flower. It arranges well
with blue, pink and mauve blooms, though one
yellow-throated variety can also be combined with
orange and yellow flowers. Autumn and winter are
the times to find it, so consider matching it with
poppies, anemones or irises.

ANEMONE

WINDFLOWER

(A. apennina, A. blanda, A. coronaria)

(Family: *Ranunculaceae*)

The anemone is an arresting flower, with its strong,
vibrant color—red, blue, purple or pink—and its
thin, papery, poppylike petals set off by a nest of
dark stamens and a thick, leafless stem. So striking
is it that it has gathered a garland of legends. The
coronaria was thought by the Greeks to have sprung
from the blood of Adonis, mortally wounded by the
boar; some say the anemone is the "lily of the field"
referred to by Christ. The common name and the old
Greek name, which means "daughter of the wind,"
refer to the belief that the flower was opened and
closed by the breeze. In fact, it blooms with the sun,
closing at night or under cloud. Twelve to eighteen
inches (30–45 cm) tall with medium-sized blossoms,
the anemone provides a colorful highlight for all
kinds of arrangements. But catch them while you
can: They are available only from November to April,
and they are not long-lived.

ANTHURIUM

FLAMINGO PLANT
(A. andreanum)
(Family: *Araceae*)

Once you have seen the anthurium, you will never confuse it with anything else. The Greek name means "tail flower," and it is easy to see why. The whitish "tail" is, in fact, composed of hundreds of tiny blossoms. When it is combined with the red, heart-shaped spathe, the total effect is so overwhelming that it is seldom possible to arrange anthuriums with any other flower. A bowl full of these tall exotics affixed to a frog, or pin holder, makes a spectacular focal point for any room. Or for a different effect, try using one or two of the flowers with such bold-textured foliage as palmetto or ti leaves to create a spare but compelling Oriental arrangement. Imported all year long from South America and Hawaii, anthuriums seem especially appropriate at Christmas.

ANTIRRHINUM

SNAPDRAGON
RABBIT'S MOUTH
(A. majus)
(Family: *Scrophulariaceae*)

Snapdragons evoke in almost everyone a fond
nostalgia for childhood: Most of us recall pinching
the blossoms along the stem to watch the "rabbit's
mouth" open and close. Throughout the summer
and fall, snapdragons are a popular favorite in flower
markets because their long stems provide a good
vertical axis for flower arrangements and their
variety of colors (white, yellow, pink, orange and
burgundy) makes them among the most versatile of
flowers. Snapdragons are not especially long-lived,
but they are relatively inexpensive. It is difficult to
imagine any "English garden" bouquet or
arrangement without them.

ASTER

CHINA ASTER
(Callistephus chinensis)
(Family: *Compositae*)

~

For some reason, the flower that most florists and
gardeners know as aster is not really of the genus
Aster at all. The Callistephus, which everyone calls
aster or China aster, comes in numerous varieties
colored a vibrant purple, pink or blue. All consist of
a whorl of bright, coarse-textured petals set off
around a yellow center. The flowers are plentiful
during the summer and fall. They look wonderful
combined with irises, snapdragons, marigolds,
zinnias or lilies. If the arrangement calls for a stiff,
vertical form, make sure to wire the stem upright,
since the head will nod otherwise.

ASTILBE

FALSE SPIREA
FALSE GOAT'S BEARD
(A. arendsii)
(Family: *Saxifragaceae*)

❧

There are few flowers that match the feathery lightness of astilbe. Not only are the spiky, quill-like sprays attractive, but the abundant foliage—when not cut away—provides needed bulk in a mass arrangement. The flower is composed of sprays of tiny white, pink or rose-colored blossoms, which give a diaphanous, almost pointillist effect when seen from a distance. Available throughout the summer and fall, astilbe mixes well with zinnias, irises, cockscomb and chrysanthemums.

BELLS OF IRELAND

MOLUCCA BALM
SHELL FLOWER
(Molucella laevis)
(Family: *Labiatae*)

~

The calyces and blooms of bells of Ireland together
make the flower. They do for each other what
diamond earrings do for ears. The actual blossoms
are tiny and white—barely visible at all—but, set in
green, bell-shaped calyces, they cluster strikingly up
and down the flower's long stem. Bells of Ireland are
long-lived and mix with other vertical forms, like
snapdragons and tuberoses. Because of their fresh,
green color, they can also be used instead of foliage
in a mass arrangement. For winter displays, they
can even be dried.

BIRD-OF-PARADISE

STRELITZIA
(S. reginae)
(Family: *Strelitziaceae*)

~

The exotic appearance of the bird-of-paradise makes
it a showy but versatile flower. The tall
stalk—straight and leafless—is topped by a large
purple-and-orange bloom resembling the head of
some tropical bird. For a stark, contemporary look,
several may be grouped in a tall, angular container;
or in a more traditional arrangement, Strelitzia may
be combined with flowers of similar color, such as
the purple monkshood (aconitum) or the orange
Enchantment lily. They can also be used in *ikebana*,
for even when the stems are cut short, "birds" make
a dramatic statement.

BOUVARDIA

(B. longiflora)
(Family: *Rubiaceae*)

~

The best thing about bouvardia is its versatility.
Available in white, orange and red, the multiflower
head has a starburst of jasminelike blossoms on top
of a two-to-three-foot (60–90 cm) stem. The special
virtue of white bouvardia is that it is a true white
with no trace of yellow, so it is ideal for
white-on-white arrangements that contain calla or
Easter lilies, stock, tuberoses or freesias.

BRODIAEA

GRASS NUT
ITHURIEL'S SPEAR
(B. elegans, B. coronaria)
(Family: *Alliaceae*)

❧

Brodiaea is often thought to be a miniature version
of agapanthus and is actually a member of the same
family. It shares with the other flower violet-blue
clusters of tiny blossoms which sit upon slender
one-foot (30 cm) stems. Unlike agapanthus, however,
the diameter of the entire flower head is quite small,
making it an excellent accent flower or extender in
mass arrangements. The delicacy of brodiaea also
gives it just the right scale for a bud vase or nosegay.

CATTAILS

TYPHA
(T. angustifolia, T. latifolia)
(Family: *Typhaceae*)

～

The cattail's native environment is the swamp or bog, but its tall, stately appearance gives it a natural elegance that belies its humble origin. The long stalk is crowned with a velvety, clublike head composed of masses of tiny brown flowers. The tall, swordlike leaves help make marvelous Oriental arrangements. They can be folded, knotted, twisted or cut to make dramatic architectural statements. Cattails themselves are especially long-lived, and make excellent extenders in mass arrangements. Use them for an exciting accent with any of the yellow gerberas or chrysanthemums that have a dark brown center.

CELOSIA

COCKSCOMB
PLUMED COCKSCOMB
(Celosia argentea 'Cristata,' C. argentea 'Plumosa')
(Family: *Amaranthaceae*)

Celosia is available in two varieties visually quite dissimilar, but each shares bold texture, vibrant color and arresting form. The variety *Cristata*, usually referred to as cockscomb, has a showy, flat, velvety, ruffled head, almost resembling a section of coral. Of medium height, it mixes well in autumn arrangements with chrysanthemums, marigolds, asters, goldenrod and zinnias. The other form, *Plumosa*, or plumed cockscomb, has a spectacular spikey plume, similar to astilbe, but with a much more dense, coarse texture and a more brilliant color. Usually available in red or gold throughout the fall, *Plumosa* makes an excellent filler in mass arrangements and, like *Cristata*, is versatile and long-lived.

CENTAUREA

BACHELOR'S BUTTON
CORNFLOWER
BLUEBOTTLE
(C. cyanus)
(Family: *Compositae*)

～

Though cornflowers are available in pink, red, lavender and white, the vibrance of its blue variety makes this bloom unmatched in popularity by any other blue flower. (Painters once used its pigment to make cyan blue.) The thin, leafy stems are covered with gray-green foliage and topped with a round, carnationlike flower. Available chiefly during the summer months—when it grows wild in grain fields around the world—cornflowers combine well with other flowers of medium height such as irises, daisies, snapdragons, and freesias.

CHRYSANTHEMUM

SPIDER MUM
(C. indicum 'Fuji')
(Family: *Compositae*)

The spider mum combines a unique and graceful effect with the good qualities common to the chrysanthemums: reasonable price, longevity and continual availability. The large flower head is composed of tubular, threadlike petals which curve at the ends, and the stems are medium-tall. Spider mums are an excellent flower, because they have enough interest to look well in sparse, three-flower Japanese settings and at the same time are not too bold to be used in conjunction with other flowers in mass arrangements. Available in white and yellow, single- and multistem varieties, they are also among the few flowers that look attractive when dyed. The peach- and pink-tinted ones are immensely popular.

CHRYSANTHEMUM

FOOTBALL MUM
EXHIBITION MUM
(C. indicum hybrid 'Rivalry')
(Family: *Compositae*)

❦

Though football mums seem as American as apple pie, they originated, like many other chrysanthemum species, in China. The enormous flower head is composed of numerous tight, incurved petals that form a round ball-shaped flower. Their long sturdy stems topped by massive white, yellow or lavender flowers make them an excellent choice for a tall container with a large opening. The exhibition mum looks best when used without other varieties, as its appearance is too bold to accept comparison.

CHRYSANTHEMUM

(C. hybrids)
(Family: *Compositae*)

❦

All chrysanthemums originally came from China,
Japan or Korea, and the total number of hybrids
available is huge. The Japanese prefer reflexed, or
recurved, petals; the Chinese like them incurved. So
central is the mum to Japanese culture that the
country's flag represents it: The "rising sun" is
really a sixteen-petal chrysanthemum.
Spider mums and exhibition mums are only the
most striking florist's varieties of chrysanthemum.
Those represented here are less able to stand alone,
but they are among the finest and most versatile
fillers for mass arrangements. The yellow pompons
provide concentrated bursts of color, while the
so-called shasta daisy has true white petals, making
it a natural for white-on-white arrangements. The
larger hybrid mums shown here, while not as
dramatic as some, are available in almost any color
combination. They are reasonably priced and
available all year long.

DAHLIAS

(Dahlia juarezii)
(Family: *Compositae*)

❦

Dahlias are available for a relatively short period
during the late summer and fall, but their
extraordinary range of glorious colors and large, lush
flowers make them worth waiting for. Most popular
of the numerous varieties are the single-petaled
anemone types, the peony-flowered varieties and the
collarettes. Grown in virtually every shade but blue,
these brilliantly colored flowers are long-lasting and
look well massed together or combined with such
other medium-height summer flowers as asters,
zinnias, snapdragons or chrysanthemums. Curiously,
they were first brought to Europe as a food crop; the
Tunebos of Colombia still eat the plant's tubers.

DAISY

MARGUERITE DAISY
OX-EYE CHAMOMILE
(Anthemis tinctoria)
(Family: *Compositae*)

Of all flowers, the daisy is perhaps the most cheerful,
its white ray petals setting off a golden-yellow center.
Hardy and inexpensive, it is an excellent filler in
mass arrangements and highlights informal
bouquets of garden flowers. The foliage, which is
deeply cut and sometimes fragrant, withers more
quickly than the flower, so you can keep daisies
longer if you remove the foliage when it no longer
looks fresh. The Marguerite mixes with almost
any other flower but is especially beautiful with
Mercedes roses or brodiaea.

DELPHINIUM

CANDLE-DELPHINIUM
CHINESE DELPHINIUM
(D. elatum, D. grandiflorum)
(Family: *Ranunculaceae*)

Only centaurea can match the intense blue found in delphinium. Though there are white and pink varieties, the light- and dark-blue shades are the most attractive. They are so blue that people often assume the flowers have been sprayed or dyed. The lush stalks are covered with vibrant flowers whose papery petals end in a long spur or tail which protrudes from the back. Their genus name comes from the Greek for "dolphin," a fish the flowers are said to resemble. They look wonderful in naturalistic country-garden arrangements with lilies, gerberas, snapdragons or stock, and they combine well in any mixed bouquet where blue is needed.

DIANTHUS

CARNATIONS
(D. caryophyllus)
(Family: *Caryophyllaceae*)

~

The standard carnation is among the most
accessible, long-lived and inexpensive flowers. At one
time or another, most buttonholes have been graced
with its vibrant colors and sweet scent. Available in
red, white, pink and salmon shades, the 12- to
18-inch (30–45 cm) stems have a medium, rounded
flower head with slim, gray-green foliage.

EREMURUS

Foxtail Lily
Desert Candle
(E. himalaicus, E. robustus)
(Family: Liliaceae)

~

Eremurus, or foxtail lily, is a spectacular flower which makes any arrangement look impressive. The tall, dense spikes are three to four feet long (90–120 cm), bearing hundreds of tiny yellow flowers tinged with orange, which gradually open from the bottom of the stem. Like allium and agapanthus, with which they mix well, the flowers open successively, never all at once—greatly extending their useful lifespan. They look wonderful with other dramatic flowers like delphiniums or irises, and should be used when a tall vertical form is needed. More than a few might overpower an arrangement, so use them sparingly. As the older blossoms on the bottom of the stem begin to wither, they can be removed without harming the rest.

EUPHORBIA

FLOWERING SPURGE
(E. fulgens)
(Family: *Euphorbiaceae*)

Euphorbia is related to poinsettia, the showy, red flowering plant seen at Christmas, and they share a similar structure, though on a different scale. In both plants, what appear to be flower petals are really bright bracts (small leaves) which surround the tiny flower. Euphorbia cascades along willowy, arching branches, a habit that makes it very attractive in mass arrangements. The two- to three-foot (60–90 cm) stem is covered with tiny blossoms in white, yellow or red. They look wonderful trailing gracefully down the sides of a tall ceramic container or a round woven basket. Don't hesitate to use them as filler in mass arrangements, since they mix well with virtually every other flower.

FREESIA

(F. refracta hybrids)
(Family: *Iridaceae*)

~

Freesia is the florist's most beautiful contradiction.
Its light and diaphanous petals, found in saturated
shades of lavender, pink, yellow and white, stand
upright in heavy bunches on a flower stalk that
emerges from only one side of the stem. This
club-footed delicacy comes with a rich, sweet scent
that can fill a whole room with fragrance. Setting
pairs of Freesia in a bud vase—say, beside the
bed—is a pleasure in itself, since to arrange even
numbers of the stems is to create do-it-yourself
symmetry. And since the flowers are available all
year long, one can mix them with almost any other
bloom or use them as extenders in mass
arrangements, always adding fragrance together
with color. Though there may be between six and
eight flowers on a stalk, often the smallest buds
nearest the end are dormant, so don't expect all of
them to bloom. Feel free to pinch off the first bloom,
which will wither before the rest.

GERBERA

TRANSVAAL DAISY
BARBERTON DAISY
(G. jamesonii hybrids)
(Family: *Compositae*)

Though native to South Africa, large numbers of gerberas are now exported to Europe and the United States via the flower markets of The Netherlands. Sold all year long, the big, electric-hued flowers are versatile, relatively inexpensive and available in virtually any color. Single- and double-flowered varieties are equally popular, and gerbera has the unique ability to share in an elegant setting including Rubrum lilies and orchids or in a simple bouquet of garden flowers. Medium-tall, gerberas must be conditioned with their heads upright for several hours before they are sold; otherwise, the heads will nod severely. If you are planning a vertical arrangement, make sure that the gerberas have been conditioned. If they have not, the only solution—and not a very good one—is to wire them. The flowers will look fresh for many days, though they may begin to wilt if the sap clogs at the bottom of the stem. To prevent this, cut a bit from the bottom of the stems each morning.

GLADIOLUS

GLADIOLA
(Gladiolus x gandavensis)
(Family: *Iridaceae*)

The great gladiolus, its bright flowers and sword-shaped leaves climbing long stalks, is perhaps the archetypal cut flower. Many of us remember the flower from childhood, when it was taller than we were. Relatively inexpensive and long-lived, the two- to five-foot (60–150 cm) spikes are available in at least 28 different colors, making them uniquely versatile in arrangement. Glads were once used chiefly as the vertical form in mass settings or for funeral pieces, but in recent years they have become popular in contemporary arrangements as well. Ten or so gladiolus thrusting out of a fishbowl provide a colorful focal point for a modern room.

GLADIOLUS

COLVILLE GLADIOLUS
MINI-GLADIOLUS
(Gladiolus x nanus)
(Family: *Iridaceae*)

❧

There are hundreds of gladiolus hybrids, but the first
of them—and perhaps the most dramatic—was the
nanus, sometimes called *colvillei* or Colville
gladiolus. Spiky and colorful like the rest of the
genus, its stems are very much shorter, usually only
around 18 inches (45 cm), making it a natural for
smaller-scale arrangements. Several varieties, such
as the white "Nymph," have a lovely maroon
diamond that extends into the flower's throat. Also
available in pink, red and salmon shades, these
long-lived stems are often used as extenders in small
settings. For a different effect, try them cut quite
short and massed in a round container.

GLORIOSA ROTHSCHILD

GLORIOSA LILY
ROTHSCHILD LILY
(G. rothschildiana, G. superba)
(Family: *Liliaceae*)

Gloriosa lilies have a unique, contorted beauty that
never becomes tiresome. Since they grow on vines,
the slender stems are often twisted and the tips of
the leaves curl like tendrils. The flowers are several
inches in diameter, with waxy crimson and gold
petals which are so inverted that the flower looks to
be inside out. They make a startling arrangement
with yellow oncidium orchids; otherwise, they
are best displayed on their own in small sparse
arrangements or alone in bud vases.

GODETIA

SATIN FLOWER
(G. grandiflora)
(Family: *Onagraceae*)

~

Godetia is prized for its bright magenta color and thin, tissue-paper petals. Each stem is multiflowered with dense foliage all along it. Removing some of the foliage makes the smaller flowers more visible and keeps the larger ones, which tend to be quite fragile, from bruising. Available primarily in summer, they are not especially long-lived, but buy them for their color. It blends exquisitely with Rubrum lilies, gerberas, and irises. An inexpensive flower, godetia also make good filler in mass arrangements.

GYPSOPHILA

BABY'S-BREATH
(G. paniculata)
(Family: *Caryophyllaceae*)

~

Baby's-breath has been much overused;
consequently, it is much—and unjustly—maligned.
Many florists will still add a spray of gypsophila to
virtually any purchase, no matter how inappropriate,
so zealous connoisseurs will indignantly reject it.
Don't be too hasty. For those traditional, Edwardian
arrangements where a dainty, misty effect is called
for, baby's-breath is an ideal filler. The spider web of
twigs is covered with a profusion of tiny, white
blossoms which may even be dried for extended use.
A larger-flowered species, *G. elegans*, is a pleasant
compromise when you want delicacy without quite
the airy quality of baby's-breath.

HELICHRYSUM

STRAWFLOWER

EVERLASTING FLOWER

CORNFLOWER

(H. bracteatum)

(Family: *Compositae*)

~

Strawflowers can be found in the summer, but—fresh or dried—they are most popular during the fall. Providentially, they share the colors of autumn leaves—red, orange, gold, and purple—and they retain their color as they dry. The stiff flower heads are made up of whorls of tiny, pointed petals usually enclosing a fuzzy, yellow corolla. Of medium height, strawflowers look lovely in traditional combinations with other dried materials: statices, baby's-breath, cattails and oak or maple leaves. To dry the flowers, hang branches of them upside down in a cool place.

HELICONIA

WILD PLANTAIN
LOBSTER CLAW
(H. bihai)
(Family: *Heliconiaceae*)

❧

Native to tropical America, heliconia shares the
exotic jungle look of the bird-of-paradise. There are
several varieties, each having a long stalk and a
large, smooth green leaf. The flower is actually
enclosed in a bright red-and-yellow bract, which is
quite hardy and long-lived. Heliconia is not
inexpensive, but it makes a dramatic statement and
only a few are necessary to catch the weariest eye. It
is best used without other varieties of flowers, but
large tropical foliage such as palmetto or ti leaves are
a suitable accompaniment.

HYACINTHUS

HYACINTH
(H. orientalis)
(Family: *Liliaceae*)

Among the earliest of spring flowers, hyacinths are well loved because, like daffodils and crocuses, they assure us that winter is past. In the Greek Isles, brides sometimes wear wreaths of hyacinth as a symbol of new beginnings. The eight-to-twelve-inch (20–30 cm) stalks are sweetly fragrant, covered with clusters of single or double flowers all along their length. Available in blue, white, pink and yellow, they are often forced to bloom even earlier than normal and are sold in flower markets during the winter as a potted flowering plant. As cut flowers, they look handsome with tulips, irises, snapdragons and narcissus.

IRIS

FLAG

(I. reticulata, I. xiphium)

(Family: *Iridaceae*)

It is said that the iris is the flower from which the form of the French *fleur de lis* was derived, and certainly there are few flowers which share the same graceful architectural form. Named for the Greek goddess of the rainbow, irises were thought to be flowers with a great variety of color, though today they are mainly available in shades of blue, lavender, yellow or white. The swordlike foliage looks wonderful in Oriental designs, but the flower adapts well to mass arrangements as well as *ikebana*. The ten- to eighteen-inch (25–45 cm) stalks are crowned by a flower which has three upright standard petals and three horizontal or hanging falls which are often striped with yellow or purple. Some even have a fuzzy ridge or crest and are known as bearded iris. They are inexpensive and available throughout the year, but they are not long-lived.

KNIPHOFIA

RED-HOT POKER
TORCH LILY
(Kniphofia uvaria)
(Family: *Liliaceae*)

Known as either kniphofia or tritoma, the red-hot poker has a whimsical quality rarely found in a flower. Maybe for this reason they are an immense favorite of hummingbirds. The six- to eight-inch (15–20 cm) head has a mass of drooping, tubular flowers that flame out from a 12- to 14-inch (30–35 cm) leafless stem. Considered to be long-lived, their unique character makes them best suited to sparse arrangements rather than mass ones. The use of foliage such as galax or ti leaves is an attractive accent for these unique flowers.

LIATRIS

BLAZING STAR
GAYFEATHER
(L. spicata)
(Family: *Compositae*)

❧

    The fuzzy lavender blossoms of liatris are unorthodox: They open from the top of the stalk first, rather than from the bottom. The almost iridescent lavender, combined with their tall, stark, bottle-brush appearance, makes them quite special. Ranging in height from 12 to 36 inches (30–90 cm), they look best when combined with other flowers which soften their sharp lines. They are well suited to mass arrangements as extenders. Long-lived and inexpensive, they are available throughout the year.

LILAC

MAY
(Syringa Vulgaris)
(Family: *Oleaceae*)

❧

Lilacs are available for such a short time—May and
June only—that a chance to buy them should never
be missed. Nothing has quite the same sweet
fragrance, lush blossoms or pleasant associations. In
parts of Devonshire, they are simply called May.
They are usually sold in bunches for quite
inexpensive sums, so treat yourself when you can.
Rather than combining them with other flowers, fill a
bowl with nothing but two- to three-foot (60–90 cm)
lilac stems and watch the faces light up as people
enter the room. Fairly long-lived, lilacs have masses
of tiny single or double blue, lavender or white
blossoms, and heart-shaped leaves. The Greek
generic name means "flute," for the branches of
lilac were once used to make them.

LILIUM

CONNECTICUT KING & RED KNIGHT
(L. hybrids)
(Family: *Liliaceae*)

The hybrid lilies are commanding beauties, their colors vibrant and saturated, their blooms firm, recurved and symmetrical, and their unopened blossoms arrayed with a regal carelessness. Among the longest-lived of all cut flowers, they can be found in every color except blue and purple, at virtually any time of year. Varieties range in height from two to five feet (60–150 cm) and may have as few as two or as many as five flowers per stem. Two hybrids are most sought after for the purity of their hues: the yellow Connecticut King and the crimson Red Knight. Lilies are seldom cheap, but you can hardly go wrong when you buy them. They look lovely alone or in virtually any color-compatible combination.

LILIUM

ENCHANTMENT LILY
(L. 'Enchantment' hybrid)
(Family: *Liliaceae*)

❧

One of the most popular lilies, it resembles the daylilies found along American roadsides in the summer and named for the speed with which they bloom and die. The Enchantment lily, by contrast, shares the great longevity of most florist's lilies and is available all year round. Closely related hybrids are called Chinook, Jamboree and Firecracker. Each features brilliant reddish-orange flowers, erect upon their stems. Country bouquets, mass arrangements and sparse Oriental settings are all appropriate for these versatile blooms.

LILIUM

RUBRUM LILY
(L. speciosum 'Rubrum')
(Family: *Liliaceae*)

As wonderful as all lilies may be, the Rubrum is in a class by itself. It is the Rolls Royce of lilies, the Mick Jagger, the "Dr. J." A variety called Uchida has stems five feet long (150 cm), covered with buds and pendulous white flowers speckled with maroon in their throats. They give the effect of a group of dancers in mid-jump. Other members of the family—Star Gazers, Dominiques or Mercy lilies—have shorter stems and a more solid feminine beauty, the large flowers (up to six inches, 15 cm, across) tinged with a pink-and-maroon center. The pollen-coated anthers that emerge from the flower will indeed drop the orange pollen after a little while, so some people cut the anthers off. The flower itself will stay firm for ten days or even two weeks. Mix Rubrums with red or pink roses, gerberas, stock, delphiniums or monkshood.

LIMONIUM

STATICE
SEA LAVENDER
(L. sinuatum)
(Family: *Plumbaginaceae*)

Although the natural home of sea lavender, or statice,
is the meadow or salt marsh, it is cultivated as a cut
flower because it is so versatile and long-lived.
Statice grows on an erect, winged stalk, with
clusters of tiny flowers which, like freesia, rise at
right angles from their stems. Sold throughout the
year, it is available in white, blue, lavender or pink.
Statice is often used as filler in mass arrangements
instead of baby's-breath, because it has more body
but still transmits a light, airy feeling. Excellent as a
dried flower, it combines well with strawflowers
and miniature cattails.

LUPINE

LUPINUS
(L. 'Russell' hybrids)
(Family: *Leguminosae*)

❦

Lupines are native to North America, but it is the
English who made them great cultivated flowers.
George Russell, a private Yorkshire gardener,
astounded the horticultural world with his hybrid
lupines, which are unsurpassed to this day. They are
tall and shapely, set around with large, showy
flowers and attractive palmlike foliage. The tapering
flower head is covered with red, pink, blue, or yellow
blossoms that extend for more than two feet (60 cm)
along the stem. Unfortunately, they are sold only
from May to July, so enjoy them during the short
time they are available. Lupines are attractive by
themselves or combined with lilies, gerberas, irises
or snapdragons in a country arrangement.

MARIGOLD

AFRICAN MARIGOLD
(Tagetes erecta)
(Family: *Compositae*)

No red, orange or yellow summer bouquet is
complete without marigolds. Although they are
among the most common garden flowers, they are
popular in flower markets because of their vivid
gold-to-orange colors, their hardiness and their
longevity. The African marigold, one of numerous
varieties, is the most popular as a cut flower because
of its big single or double flower and its sturdy stem.
The pungent fragrance of marigolds is agreeable to
some people but too strong for others: Gardeners
often plant them around vegetables, as the
scent is thought to repel insects. Marigolds look
wonderful when combined with chrysanthemums,
zinnias, or cockscomb.

MONKSHOOD

WOLF'S-BANE
(Aconitum napellus)
(Family: *Ranunculaceae*)

The deadly juice of monkshood was once used as a
sedative and even for arrow poison, but we value the
plant today for its delicate ornamental flower. The
blossom has a rich, blue color and a hooded shape,
while the foliage—dark green and deeply cut—has
ornamental value in itself. The flower's long spikes
are two or three feet (60–90 cm) high with numerous
small flowers all along the stem. It arranges well
with other tall flowers such as bird-of-paradise, lilies,
snapdragons and mums. Fairly long-lived,
monkshood is available throughout the spring
and summer.

NARCISSUS

DAFFODIL
JONQUIL
(Narcissus sp. various)
(Family: *Amaryllidaceae*)

～

Named for the Greek youth Narcissus, whose admiration of his own beauty caused the gods to turn him into a flower nodding at the water's edge, the genus Narcissus contains the most classic of all spring flowers. The ones called daffodils are usually of the trumpet-shaped variety, but because of hybridization, one is likely to find all members of the genus called simply narcissus. The clusters of smaller white blooms are often called jonquils. The upthrusting green leaves and the erect stem topped with nodding white, orange or yellow flowers give all the narcissus a cheerful demeanor. In parts of England, they call the yellow-and-white narcissus "Butter and Eggs." Tulips, irises, oncidium orchids and snapdragons make pleasant partners for these heralds of spring.

NERINE

CAPE COLONY NERINE
(N. bowdenii)
(Family: *Amaryllidaceae*)

The flower takes its name from *nereid*, or sea nymph. The group of pink blooms straining upward as though pulling their green stems behind them must have reminded some botanist of nymphs jumping from the waves. The nerine's flowers, like those of agapanthus, open one at a time, so if you are patient, you will get to enjoy a flower that unfolds gracefully and lasts for quite a while. The iridescent pink blooms arrange elegantly with Rubrum lilies, gerberas, monkshood or alstroemerias.

ORCHID

ARACHNIS
(Arachnis hybrids)
(Family: *Orchidaceae*)

Among the smaller orchids, arachnis are the most versatile. Each spray is 12 to 24 inches (30–60 cm) long and covered with a number of small, spidery flowers. Alone in a bud vase they look quite elegant, but they are not too dramatic to mix well with other flowers. The golden arachnis with maroon spots or stripes is a particularly good mixer. Try it with orange or yellow lilies, gerberas or mums.

ORCHID

CYMBIDIUM
(Cymbidium hybrids)
(Family: *Orchidaceae*)

As popular as cattleyas, cymbidiums have a truly
exquisite appearance and are available in many
colors. The large flowers grow in foot-long (30 cm)
sprays with numerous blossoms along the stem.
Lilies and orchids seem to have a natural affinity for
each other, so a mass arrangement containing the
two is not only impressive but will easily last for two
weeks. Like cattleyas, cymbidiums have been used
frequently in corsages, but they adapt well to
ikebana settings. And just one spray looks quite
lovely in a tall, narrow container or bud vase.

ORCHID

CATTLEYA, DENDROBIUM & ONCIDIUM
(C., D. & O. hybrids)
(Family: *Orchidaceae*)

Orchids make up the second-largest family in the
plant kingdom, numbering more than 18,000
species. Of all the cultivated species and their
hybrids, the cattleyas are among the most showy.
The large, yellow-throated white cattleya (shown
here) and its striking mauve relative are what people
think of most often when they think of orchids. Once
the cattleya was used almost exclusively for
corsages, but it is very attractive in sparse
three-flower arrangements. The medium-small
dendrobiums give an equally elegant but much more
relaxing effect. The foot-long (30 cm) sprays are
dotted with numerous purple, white or
white-and-lavender flowers. They make a lovely
free-form cascade, trailing down the sides of a
container or arching gracefully from a fishbowl. Tiny
oncidiums combine the airiness of baby's-breath
with the showiness of the orchid family. They add a
frothy, light dimension to any bouquet, arranging
particularly well with gloriosa rothschild.

ORNITHOGALUM

STAR-OF-BETHLEHEM
CHINCHERINCHEE
(O. thyrsoides)
(Family: *Liliaceae*)

Chincherinchee or star-of-Bethlehem bear pointed
stalks of six to twelve white, star-shaped flowers
which have a delicacy that lends itself to Oriental
settings, though they can also be used successfully
as extenders in mass arrangements. Of medium
height, star-of-Bethlehem is an extremely long-lasting
flower which opens slowly and is available
throughout the year. In Britain, it is especially
popular at Christmas, when it is imported from
South Africa. Relatively inexpensive, it combines well
with amaryllis, gerberas or other brightly colored
flowers. For an interesting white-on-white
arrangement, try them with white freesias, stock,
calla lilies and baby's-breath in a silver
or pewter container.

PEONY

(Paeonia lactiflora)
(Family: *Paeoniaceae*)

Most of us enjoy the same pleasant childhood association with peonies that we have with lilacs and snapdragons. A common garden flower, peonies are now a very popular cut flower in most flower markets during the spring. Apart from their sweet fragrance, they are much desired for their large flowers, glossy foliage and long stems. Peonies are not long-lived, but their lush flowers and lovely aroma make them hard to resist.

PHLOX

(P. paniculata, P. carolina)
(Family: *Polemoniaceae*)

~

Phlox is an early-summer flower, with a showy pink,
white, rose, or lavender head composed of hundreds
of small, individual blossoms. Sometimes, the
blooms have a dark blush at their centers. The
medium-to-long stems are sturdy and quite leafy. It
is usually a good idea to remove the leaves close to
the flower head, so the blossoms stand out clearly.
Phlox is short-lived but relatively inexpensive, so
buying it really isn't an extravagance. It contrasts
pleasantly in arrangements with more dramatic
flowers like snapdragons, irises and tulips.

PHYSALIS

CHINESE LANTERNS
WINTER CHERRY
(P. alkekengi. P. franchetti)
(Family: *Solanaceae*)

~

Unlike most cut flowers, physalis is not valued for its
flower or its foliage but earns its popularity for the
pleasing shape and vibrant color of its seed pod. The
bright orange seed coverings look like miniature
Chinese lanterns, and they dangle delicately from the
branches on small, arching stems. Usually the
florist will remove the foliage for you, to give the
"lanterns" maximum visibility. The stems are over a
foot long (30 cm), so they make wonderful extenders
in autumn arrangements, combined with either
fresh-cut or dried flowers. Chinese lanterns
themselves can be dried and used over
and over again.

PINCUSHION FLOWER

SCABIOSA
(S. caucasica, S. atropururea)
(Family: *Dipsaceae*)

❧

Scabiosa was once thought to cure itching—hence its
unattractive generic name—but today we value it for
its fragile flower. Its parchment petals, sweet
fragrance and longevity make the pincushion flower
a popular favorite. The flowers range in color from
one sort which is nearly black to one which is white,
but the most common colors are blue, pink, lavender,
salmon and red. The ruffled petals
spread like a petticoat around a center of silvery
stamens which look like a pincushion, giving the
flower its common name. Of medium height,
scabiosas are ideal matches for irises, Rubrum lilies
and shasta daisies.

POPPY

PAPAVER
(P. orientale, P. nudicaule)
(Family: *Papaveraceae*)

～

The poppy's beauty, like the anemone's, is
otherworldly, even sinister. The bright and gossamer
petals spread wide, cradling a burr of short stamens.
The large flowers are yellow or orange in the
Icelandic variety, but the Oriental poppy, the opium
poppy, is a brilliant red or pink with a mound of
black stamens in the center. Available for a short
period in the early spring, poppies do not live long.
To improve their longevity, sear the end of each stem
with a match and place it in warm water
before arranging.

PROTEA

KING PROTEA

PINCUSHION PROTEA

(Protea cynaroides, Leucospermum cordifolium)

(Family: *Proteaceae*)

❧

Protea are among those rare specimen flowers that
need no accompaniment and can never be mistaken
for anything else, except perhaps an alien being.
Among the most popular varieties are the
Pincushion protea, a one- to one-and-a-half-foot
(30–45 cm), thick woody stalk topped with a
five-inch (12 cm), bright orange flower head. The
bloom is composed of petals which have the shape
and texture of pine needles. King protea (shown here)
and its smaller cousin, called Pink Mink, are equally
interesting, blessed with good color, exotic form and
interesting texture. The King protea has a
grapefruit-sized pink head with prickly artichoke-like
petals that are covered with velvety down. The
smaller variety has the same soft pink color, but its
gentler petals have black tips. One or two protea in a
vase with a tropical leaf, such as ti or palmetto, look
lovely, but if you choose to combine them with other
flowers, use something as bold as heliconia.

ROSES

(Rosa hybrids)
(Family: *Rosaceae*)

❦

There is scarcely a culture in the world that doesn't know the rose. The most important discoveries made about roses in recent years, apart from hybridization, have to do with their care: The annoying tendency of cut roses to nod on the stem can be prevented by recutting the stems *under water*. Another, more traditional way to prolong the life of a rose is to avoid exposing it to direct sunlight or heat.

Excellent red roses are the American Beauty (top), which has a lovely scent and a clear red color, and the Mercedes (bottom left), with its cabbage-shaped head, bright orange-red color and outstanding longevity. Sonia (top left) is the most well known and attractive of the roses in the pink or peach family. The Sweetheart rose (bottom right), a small-flowered, short-stemmed variety, is inexpensive and lends itself well to mixed arrangements. Yellow and white roses are also good mixers. Try white roses in arrangements with other whites: tuberoses, ornithogalums, baby's-breath or shasta daisies.

SOLIDAGO

GOLDENROD

(S. canadensis)

(Family: *Compositae*)

❧

Goldenrod is one of the few cut flowers thought of as
a mixed blessing. Valued for its showy yellow flower,
it has been used for medicinal purposes and as a
source for yellow dye. On the other hand, many
people are allergic to the pollen. If it doesn't cause
you or your friends health problems, you will find it
is a lovely late-summer flower. Try it in combination
with zinnias, marigolds and chrysanthemums.
The six- to twelve-inch (15–30 cm) stems are
covered with many linear clusters of tiny golden
blossoms, making goldenrod an excellent filler
in mass arrangements.

STOCK

BROMPTON STOCK
(Mathiola incana)
(Family: *Cruciferae*)

❧

The pungent, spicy aroma of stock evokes visions of evening in an Oriental paradise. The fragrance seems to increase as the sun goes down. The richly scented flowers—available in purple, lavender or white—grow on woody stalks with the blossoms massed toward the top. Available primarily during the summer months, it is fairly long-lived. To preserve stock a bit longer, smash the bottom of the stems instead of cutting them.

THISTLE

GLOBE THISTLE & SCOTCH THISTLE
(Echinops ritro & Onoppordon bracteatum)
(Family: *Compositae*)

Globe thistle makes a dynamic display. As it ages, it seems to increase in interest. The medium, gray-blue flower head is cut while the myriad tiny blossoms that comprise its head are in bud; as they open, the tight iridescent ball of blue becomes an eye-catching cluster. The stems are of medium height and the leaves are a shiny green with a spiny texture. The Onoppordon, or Scotch thistle, has a more elongated, globular head with eerie, sinuous tentacles surrounding it. Thistles retain their attractive appearance when dried, so hold on to them for dried as well as fresh-cut arrangements.

TUBEROSE

POLIANTHES
(P. tuberosa)
(Family: *Agavaceae*)

Tuberoses are without exception the most fragrant of all flowers sold. Perhaps the most odorous rose is sweeter, but you won't find it in the flower market. As a matter of fact, the essential oils from specially selected hybrids of both tuberoses and roses are used to make costly perfumes. Both double- and single-flower tuberoses are scented. The double flower, which is white with a pink tinge, has a much stiffer vertical habit, while the pure white single variety tends to nod. Both varieties are medium-tall, covered with lovely jasminelike blossoms; both will last for a week or more and can be bought throughout the year. They are not inexpensive, but you need only a few to turn a bouquet into a sweet delight.

TULIP

(Tulipa gesneriana hybrids)
(Family: *Liliaceae*)

Among the most familiar of flowers, the tulip's limpid form and clear, bright color make it a universal favorite. Though not long-lived, tulips are generally inexpensive and are now available the year round. The spectrum of colors and varieties is unparalleled, since tulip breeding and hybridization have been a major Dutch industry since the seventeenth century. In 1634, at the height of Dutch tulipomania, rare varieties sold for up to 5,500 florins. (That's about £1,500 or $2,500, a fortune in those days.) Today the Dutch alone claim over 10,000 varieties. Tulips combine well with virtually all of the spring bulbs: iris, narcissus, hyacinth or lily. Red, orange, yellow, pink and white were always the most popular colors, but new varieties are variegated and extremely showy. The waxy flower head opens gradually, revealing a wonderful purply-black center which heightens the effect of the colorful petals.

YARROW

ACHILLEA
(A. filipendulina)
(Family: *Compositae*)

~

Yarrow has a modern, minimalist beauty that lends
itself to both mass and sparse Oriental
arrangements. A group of yarrow looks like a tiny
grove of tropical trees. The long, arrow-straight
stem has attractive fernlike leaves and
mustard-colored flowers that group in quiltlike
mounds at the top of the stalk. Yarrow dries perfectly
and looks well when combined with fresh or dried
cattails, strawflowers and statice.

ZANTEDESCHIA

CALLA LILY
ARUM LILY
LILY OF THE NILE
(Z. aethiopica)
(Family: *Araceae*)

The large, trumpet-shaped blossom of the calla lily is
pristine-white. Some specimens give the effect of
blown glass; others, of porcelain or polished marble.
From the center of the sinuous petal—perhaps to
keep the flower from taking itself *too* seriously—rises
a bright yellow spadix. All of this seriocomic display
is propped on a stout stem over two feet (60 cm)
high. Callas are such an event in themselves that it
is difficult to think of combining them with other
flowers, but, if you must, keep the arrangement stark
and architectural or sparse and Oriental.

ZINNIAS

YOUTH-AND-AGE
(*Z. elegans*)
(Family: *Compositae*)

Zinnias are among the most common garden flowers, blooming from early summer to late autumn. They are also excellent cut flowers and should not be missed. Zinnias come in yellow, orange, red and pink, with multicolored and striped varieties. The large flowers have slightly coarse but vibrantly colored petals in both single and double varieties. Zinnias are best for informal country bouquets or arrangements, combined with chrysanthemums, irises, marigolds or statice.